I Hope You Die Laughing

A Beginner's Guide to Estate Planning

by N. M. Harvey

Published by N. M. Harvey, Reno, Nevada

Printed by CreateSpace, An Amazon.com Company
Available from Amazon.com, CreateSpace.com, and other retail outlets.

First printing, November 2014.
Second Edition, April 2015.

ISBN-13: 978-1511832304
ISBN-10: 1511832304
Copyright © 2014 by N. M. Harvey. All rights reserved.

People plan, God laughs.

TABLE OF CONTENTS

Introduction 1
Chapter 1: What Is An Estate Plan? 6
Chapter 2: A Will is a Dead Giveaway 10
Chapter 3: Trusting 17
Chapter 4: The Game of Favorites 23
Chapter 5: Best Friends 33
Chapter 6: Digital Property 40
Chapter 7: Declaration of Authority 44
Chapter 8: Financial Powers of Attorney 48
Chapter 9: Healthcare Powers of Attorney 56
Chapter 10: Living Will 68
Chapter 11: Signed & Sealed 71
Appendix: Estate Plan Worksheet 76
Glossary 81

INTRODUCTION

> Major Burns: Can't you ever be serious?
>
> Captain Pierce: I tried it once, but everybody laughed.
>
> *M*A*S*H: Dear Dad, Again (#1.18) (1973)*

Humor, like any other weapon, is as dangerous as it can be protective. The difficult topics must be seriously considered, sometimes reverently, and approached with solemnity and gravitas. At the same time, there is no use in becoming so wallowed in the seriousness of merely potential circumstances that may never come to pass that we forget to enjoy the vast miracle of the present moment in which we *have* the capacity, the knowledge and the awareness to consider such decisions.

I decided to write this little book when I realized

that I had all but memorized my "lines" in my meetings to review and sign estate plan documents with my clients. Some of my lines are quite funny, and it's that way for a reason; we're talking about becoming incapacitated and dying. It's uncomfortable and unsettling at best; it's downright depressing at worst. As an attorney, and as an economist, I care quite a lot that my clients understand the choices they have to make, and that they have as much accurate information as possible with which to make their choices. As a human, I understand that feelings often get in the way of understanding, and in the way of reason. That's why I use humor.

  I live in a nice little suburban neighborhood, on a tucked away little street where nothing much seems to ever happen. Once, a couple streets over, a little kid was struck by a car and killed in a crosswalk. His older brother had seen it happen. My daughter's elementary school had a book fair not long after. I was perusing the shelves with my daughter, when I heard a young boy's voice pipe up just a touch louder than the conversational din, "Do you want to know what's funny about my brother dying?"

Conversations stopped. I turned to look, with the rest of the parents, mostly mothers, to see the young boy who spoke, standing with his mother, near his siblings, talking with a teacher. I held my breath for him. I had thought about that older brother quite a lot after I'd heard the story; wondered what he saw, what he remembered, how he was dealing with it. Whether he had resources to deal with it. Whatever he was going to say, it would probably make me cry a little, but I hoped for us both he was already reaching at humor to get him through. "When the car hit him, it took him out of his shoes. And no one ever found them."

The teacher jumped in, "You mean funny, strange,

not funny like a joke."

The boy looked down, "Yeah."

Death, dying and incapacity are sensitive topics, and I certainly don't joke around with every client in the same way. Some people are really not open to humor, and that's OK with me too. Behind my humor is the respect and civility this topic demands.

Of course, I also have to warn you that this little book does not constitute legal advice; you should consult an attorney for advice that applies to your particular situation.

I hope you find this is a good translation from Legalese to English, and I hope you learn something helpful along the way. And I hope it makes you laugh, at least once.

Lorem ipsum (Enjoy).

WHEN I DIE

WILL SOMEONE PLEASE
GO TO MY FUNERAL
DRESSED LIKE THE
GRIM REAPER?
DON'T SAY ANYTHING,
JUST STAND THERE...

CHAPTER 1:

WHAT IS AN ESTATE PLAN?

> A woman walked into her attorney's office asking for an estate plan. He said he would be happy to assist her, but he required a $5,000 retainer. She wrote the check and gave it to him. He thanked her and asked her to tell him about her estate.
>
> She replied, "You just took it."

An estate plan is a set of documents designed to address the issues that arise when you can't make decisions for yourself – like if you become incapacitated, or if you pass away. It's probably more accurately described as a "family protection plan," since most of us don't fancy ourselves as having "estates." Most people find it very difficult to discuss and prepare an estate plan, because it requires taking a hard look at the terrible situations that could befall them, and the people they love the most. Sometimes folks have the comfort of realizing they have someone they trust to look after them in bad times. Sometimes it's a big, hard reality check. There is a huge psychological benefit in the planning; I've heard from hundreds of clients they feel relieved when we're done because they feel they are finally prepared for the worst that could happen.

When I think about, or talk about, an "estate plan," I consider the basic documents first: maybe a trust, maybe a will, the appointment of someone to handle funeral arrangements, a financial power of attorney, a healthcare power of attorney, a HIPAA release, and a living will. There may be more involved in the plan; maybe a Declaration of Homestead, real estate deeds, or other agreements.

An estate plan is something different for everyone;

they are just as unique as the people who plan them, and there is no hard and fast recipe about how to make one (no matter what the Internet tells you). I once worked for a lawyer who always said, "A template is a good place to start, but it won't be a template when you're finished." That's the value of knowledgeable legal counsel in estate planning; a lawyer who knows what they're doing can help tailor your estate plan perfectly for your needs.

The whole idea behind estate planning is to have considered and planned for certain circumstances over which you otherwise would not have any control, in order to make life a little easier for your caretakers and survivors.

Woody: Guys, guys, we all knew this time would come.

Mr. Potato Head: Yeah, but now it's here!

~Toy Story 3 (2010)

CHAPTER 2:

A WILL IS A DEAD GIVEAWAY

> "To my first wife Sue, whom I always promised to mention in my will. Hello Sue!"
>
> Anthony Scott's Last Will & Testament

A Will is a document that is witnessed and authenticated, and distributes property by written instructions, according to the pleasure of its maker.

Wills as we understand and use them today began even before the English Statute of Wills in the year 1540. For centuries, people of means have relied on wills to transfer their property upon their death. Shakespeare left a will; so did George Washington, Benjamin Franklin, Janis

Joplin and Walt Disney.

If you want your property to be distributed outright to your chosen beneficiary/beneficiaries without any further specificity, then a Will may be for you. Once a Will is done, it is done, and it can be put on a shelf until you want to look at it again. A will is simple to revoke or change, and you don't have to change the way you handle your personal business (like you would with a trust).

Some would say that, with a will, you are destined for probate, and that probate must be avoided at all costs. There are two things you should know about that: (1) having a will doesn't necessarily mean there will be a probate; (2) probate is not as scary or expensive as it's made out to be. So what is a probate?

Probate is the name of a legal process that is used to transfer assets that belong to a person who is deceased. Through the probate process, the executor of a will is legally granted authority to handle the deceased person's affairs, sell and liquidate their assets, and distribute their stuff to their beneficiaries. If the deceased person didn't have a Will, the Court might appoint an administrator to handle the estate, and distribute according to "intestacy" or "intestate succession". The probate court oversees the process, resolves disputes, and enforces deadlines to move the process forward. Probate courts and probate rules have existed as long as wills have, and though every state has its own rules, it's quite similar across the country. The probate process anticipates and has a method for resolving disputed property among heirs and beneficiaries; and sometimes there is a benefit to having a judge intervene if you anticipate there may be some disagreement in the wake of your death.

In Nevada, there are different levels of probate process depending on the size of the estate. Estates under

$20,000 do not require any court process. Estates worth more than $20,000 but less than $100,000 do not require any probate process, except for a petition asking the Court to review what assets are in the estate, and approve of your plan for distribution, without any oversight after the one petition. Estates worth $100,000 to $200,000 get "Summary Administration" which is a short version of "General Administration." General Administration is for all estates over $200,000.

And this is where the "game" of avoiding probate begins: regardless of whether or not you have a will, if your estate has $20,000 or less, your heirs will be able to avoid probate.

How do we determine what is in your estate? Any assets titled to you are in your estate. Assets titled to you but for which you have designated a beneficiary upon your death will not pass through your estate. This doesn't work for everyone: it depends on what you have and how you want to pass it on. But if it can work for you, you can have complete control over how assets are distributed, and your heirs will not have any "process" to deal with in order to receive something from you. In Nevada, real estate can be transferred outside an estate through a deed called a "Beneficiary Deed" or "Transfer on Death Deed." Nevada's DMV has a form that will allow a person to designate a beneficiary of their vehicle for just $20. Bank accounts can have a "Pay on Death" or "Transfer on Death" order; it's usually a deposit slip-sized form that you can complete at the teller counter. Investment accounts, life insurance policies, retirement accounts can all have designated beneficiaries. If you're able to designate everything the way you want it, your will becomes your "just-in-case" backup plan.

With a will, you can still protect gifts to underage

beneficiaries with the power of a trust. As discussed in detail in the next chapter, sometimes trusts are necessary. We use "springing trusts" that allow us to appoint someone else to manage and distribute a share to a minor child with specific instructions. It's called a "springing" trust because the trust is dormant until it's needed. When it is time to distribute a share to a minor, the trust springs to life, affording your beneficiary and their trustee the powers and protections of operating through a trust.

Careful estate planning includes evaluating what kind of document best suits your needs to dispose of your unique assets. For a lot of people, a carefully drafted will is all they need, and they won't even need that if their assets pass through beneficiary designations.

An elderly gentleman had serious hearing problems for a number of years. He went to the doctor and the doctor was able to have him fitted for a set of hearing aids that allowed the gentleman to hear 100%.

The elderly gentleman went back in a month to the doctor and the doctor said: "Your hearing is perfect. Your family must be really pleased that you can hear again."

The gentleman replied, "Oh, I haven't told my family yet. I just sit around and listen to their conversations. I've changed my will three times!"

CHAPTER 3:

TRUSTING

A trust is a device whereby a trustee manages property for one or more beneficiaries. Trusts became popular for basic "Mom & Pop" estate planning at a time when the federal government taxed transfers between spouses on relatively small estates. Very smart people realized trusts were a way to preserve assets for a surviving spouse and future generations, and avoid the tax.

Trusts are great for a lot of things. Anytime you want to continue controlling your money long after you're gone, or if you have an estate the size of which is subject to estate tax, a trust can help you solve your problem. Trusts are great for underage beneficiaries, to control how and when they receive their money from you, and how they can use it. They are great for ongoing support of an important cause or organization. In some circumstances, trusts can even be used to protect ownership of dangerous firearms.

Every now and then, a surviving spouse will come visit me when their loved one passes away to ask what needs to be done. If they have a properly funded trust, the answer is typically "nothing." The relief from such a burden is remarkable, and well worth the planning for your surviving spouse.

Trusts are also high maintenance vehicles. Once you've created a trust, you must be aware of the way you buy and sell things in your name, or the trust's name, and the way you handle your accounts. It may or may not change the way you designate beneficiaries on life insurance and other accounts, and either way, you need to consider those funds through the process. Amendments may be necessitated by state or federal law changes, and you should keep a close relationship with your attorney (and keep your attorney's retainer account full) as the trust continues.

Raisin cookies that look like chocolate chip cookies are the reason I have trust issues

Trusts can do amazing, sometimes even magical, things. They can help you avoid taxable situations, and they can even let you control your property long after you're dead. They can protect assets from creditors who want to make a beneficiary satisfy their debts. They can provide a source of money without offsetting disability benefits for disabled and elderly beneficiaries.

But there is always a trade-off.

If you want the highest and best protection possible from a trust, you will have to actually TRUST a third party to serve as co-trustee. Many people choose their CPA, their attorney, or trusted financial advisor for this role. If you're willing and able to trust a third party trustee, Nevada offers extraordinary powers to protect your assets, only matched by complicated and expensive offshore instruments. Nevada is a great jurisdiction for trust-related planning. I read one estate planner brag that to get a trust with stronger protections, you'd have to go offshore for a Cayman Islands Trust. I'm not sure what he based his opinion on, but I sure do like to repeat it. If you're willing and able to trust a third party trustee, you can ensure a better quality of life for your beneficiaries, for a longer period of time.

It's not just your trustee that you have to be able to trust; you have to be able to trust the beneficiaries as well. In Nevada, as in most jurisdictions, beneficiaries have certain rights with respect to the trust, in addition to the rights they might receive in the written instrument.

Trustees have certain obligations to the beneficiaries and to you as the creator, or "Settlor" of the trust. An irresponsible beneficiary can drain trust funds by constant objection to the trustee's administration, and can even request that a court exercise jurisdiction over the administration of the trust by the trustee.

Nevada allows trusts to exist for 365 years. We have "spendthrift trusts," and credit shelter trusts, to keep assets from judgment creditors, and you can even be your own co-trustee of such a trust. Depending on what you have to protect, and who you have to protect it from or for, Nevada might be the place for you to prepare your estate plan. You don't have to be a Nevada resident to enjoy the benefits of

a Nevada trust.

> A woman goes into the local newspaper office to see that the obituary for her recently deceased husband is published. After the editor informs her that the fee for the obituary is 50 cents a word, she pauses, reflects and then says, "Well, then, let it read, 'Fred Brown died.'"
>
> Confounded at the woman's thrift, the editor stammers that there is a 7-word minimum for all obituaries. The woman pauses again, counts on her fingers and replies, "In that case, 'Fred Brown died: 1983 Pick-up for sale.'"

CHAPTER 4:

THE GAME OF FAVORITES

> A woman in Brooklyn decided to prepare her Will and final wishes. She told her attorney she had two final requests. First, she wanted to be cremated, and second, she wanted her ashes scattered all over Macy's.
>
> "Why Macy's?" asked the attorney.
>
> "Then I'll be sure my daughters visit me twice a week."

My Great Grandma Schatz was a special woman who came into my life with my stepdad. She was German; you could still hear an accent from her in her 80s, although she spent her life in America. Grandpa Eddie died before I knew her, and everyone remembered him so fondly, most especially Grandma.

Grandma shared a little secret with each and every grandchild and great-grandchild. Only God knows how she kept track of all those special memories and secrets, and remembered them every time she saw us.

We used to drive to Stockton from Arizona to see Grandma Schatz every Christmas or Thanksgiving that we could. Her house would be so full of sleeping bags and air mattresses; whispering and giggling and story-telling, all about the house. All except for Grandma's room, where she managed to sleep in her twin bed, next to grandpa's empty twin bed.

The best thing about Great Grandma Schatz was that everyone thought they were her favorite. The thing was, all of us, for three generations after her, had such evidence - mountains of it - and each believed we were her favorite.

I was almost twenty when Grandma Schatz passed away. No one really considered me an adult yet, and I wasn't much privy to the conversations about her estate. The night before her funeral, we stayed at her house, among sleeping bags and air mattresses. There wasn't a lot of whispering, and no giggling that night.

After her funeral, there was a big discussion among my parents and grandparents about cousins and other cousins and a disagreement about who would get the water pump. Grandma's backyard featured an amazing old-fashioned well water pump. The story about Grandma's water pump was that when she moved with her family from Kansas to California during the Great Depression, each child was allowed to bring one thing, and Grandma wanted the pump. She had it ever since.

The other skirmish I remember was over the closet door. Grandma's hall closet door was normal from the outside, but on the inside, every grandchild and great-grandchild had measured their height, and marked the date and their name for years and years and years.

Looking back, it really was a shame there was any acrimony or dispute over Grandma Schatz's things. But Grandma never wanted anyone to have hurt feelings, and it's impossible to imagine her making lists of people to be in charge, and people to receive property. Some people don't want to play favorites, and ultimately cause problems with their heirs.

"Playing favorites" is something we all do, have been accused of doing, have accused someone of doing, and have denied doing. Wills and Trusts are often instruments that demonstrate the winners and losers of the Game of Favorites; we see it in the distribution, and all too often with the choice of executor. When we're talking about the choice of executor or trustee, "favorites" is a terrible framework for decision-making.

There are a lot of people like my Grandma Schatz; they have big, sweet, loving hearts, and don't leave any written instruction, hoping to avoid an argument between others. They think choosing an executor means ranking their favorite relatives, and they don't want to hurt anyone's feelings. But writing down what you want isn't actually enough; sometimes, you also have to say what you don't want.

The person appointed to carry out the instructions of a will is the "executor." That's ex-EK-u-tor, not EX-e-cu-tor. A trustee is appointed by a trust, and similarly carries out the instructions in the trust. The person you choose should be more than just "responsible;" they should be honest, reliable and be able to see a project through to the end.

Some people assume the worst that could happen

with a bad choice of executor is an executor stealing from the estate. It's actually not that simple to abscond with estate assets in today's world; there's a worse kind of fallout from a bad appointment. The worst that happens is when an executor wastes the estate through inaction or slow action.

In one such case, the woman who made the will named three of her four adult children as executor and backup executors. The estate was to be divided among all four equally. The child left out of the executor succession drove the other three nuts with his obsession over not being named as executor, so much so that all three said they wanted nothing to do with the estate, and one even disclaimed his share. The fourth child came to be in charge of the small estate, which was anticipated to net $40,000 to each beneficiary. He took months to clean out the residence and list the house. He refused to recarpet and paint – not for lack of funds, but because he "didn't want to get involved in all that." When the sale of the filthy, tobacco-stained house closed and the estate was distributed, there was slightly more than $2,000 for each beneficiary. The estate was wasted supporting estate property for too long before the distribution. Mom knew better than to name her fourth child, but she didn't specifically exclude him.

In another case, a father also had three choices for executor and backups: his friend, his bank and his lawyer, all of whom were unable or unwilling when called upon to serve. The man's only son, a drug abuser and felon, petitioned the court for permission to handle the estate. Although most states don't allow felons to serve as executors, the court made exception in this case because no one objected. Months went by in a process that should have taken just weeks. Ultimately, it took the pressure of his attorney, the court, and another lawyer for a beneficiary for the distribution to be done accurately. Dad knew better than to name his son as executor, but he didn't specifically exclude the son.

When people address the distribution of their estates, they certainly don't mind identifying those persons who would not receive anything under any circumstances, if that's their desire. Most estate planners will use an "Omitted Heirs" clause in their Wills and Trusts. Roughly translated from Legalese, it says if you left someone out of your plan, you left them out on purpose, and it was not an accident. It usually goes on to say if such a person objects to your plan, that they receive nothing from your estate. But when people choose executors, I often see uneasiness from parents who don't want anyone to feel left out or to have hurt feelings. Very often – more than most parents would like to admit – parents have a child or children they don't necessarily trust to carry out their wishes. "Well, if we go in birth order, then she'll be last, and that's not too likely, and that way she won't feel left out." Estate planning is not about what's "likely" and it's never about making anyone feel good about themselves; it is about every possible contingency, likely or unlikely. It's a belt and suspenders, and a rope just like Jethro and Elly May.

Perhaps the upset will be unavoidable. If you know there will be hurt feelings, plan for it. There are many ways to force people to get their emotions out of the way in order for you to have your wishes met. One of the best arbiters is time. Most wills or trusts make the heirs wait thirty days for a distribution. If you know there will be fighting, make it longer. Ninety days, for example, is quite a long time for heirs to wait for a distribution, and during that time they can work out their aggressions, their emotions, speak their peace, say their minds, and maybe even have the last word. It's your estate plan; you could make them wait 30 days, 90 days, 1,000 days; it's up to you. And no one knows your heirs better than you do. If you think they'll need the extra time, give them time to cool off before anyone can get anything.

You and your heirs will be much better off choosing a person well-suited for the office of Trustee or Executor, rather than assuaging anger by just "not mentioning." Perhaps your favorite child is not your favorite for executor; that's OK. You have to play favorites when you're choosing the person or people who will carry out your instructions, based on the requirements of the job. When you choose an executor or trustee who will play by the rules, everyone wins.

CHAPTER 5:

BEST FRIENDS

> F. I leave the sum of Twelve Million Dollars ($12,000,000.00) to the Trustees of the LEONA HELMSLEY JULY 2005 TRUST, established under an instrument dated on or about the date of this Will, to be disposed of in accordance with the provisions of that Trust agreement. I leave my dog, Trouble, if she survives me, to my brother, ALVIN ROSENTHAL, if he survives me or if he does not survive me, to my grandson, DAVID PANZIRER. I direct that when my dog, Trouble, dies, her remains shall be buried next to my remains in the Helmsly Mausoleum at Woodlawn Cemetery, Bronx, New York, or in such other mausoleum as I may be interred pursuant to this Will.
>
> Leona Helmsly's Will

I listened to the screams in the background while the caller frantically explained to the 911 operator that a young woman was being viciously attacked by a dog. I had to listen to it more than once to know exactly what was said. I worked for the lawyer representing the young woman, who survived, but was permanently disfigured and disabled from the incident.

The dogs, it turned out, were not first offenders; they'd attacked before. Much like their owners, who were repeat misdemeanor offenders and frequent arrestees. The dog owners owned a junkyard, where they also lived, and the dogs were their security system. The dogs were raised to be hostile, vicious and mean. As the case progressed, it became obvious the animals were a perfect mirror of their environment.

My dog at the time was a loyal, all-of-10-lbs., Italian Greyhound named Victor. Victor Thomas, actually. You have to give something two names at least, so it can know when it's in trouble. He was a snuggler, as small dogs are, and he was very smart. When I was working for the legal department of an international pet retailer, he came to work with me nearly every day. He had a little collar and tie that went around his neck, so he'd at least be dressed properly, and his black and white markings helped with that.

Victor loved to be outside, loved really long walks, and loved taking naps in front of a weekend baseball game. He was a perfect mirror of his environment.

Isn't that the conventional wisdom? Dogs are "man's [and women's] best friend." I saw a National Geographic documentary about how dogs can interpret human expressions. Victor certainly knew my habits better than I did. I've always been a little forgetful, and it was common for me to turn around and go back into my apartment for something after I'd locked it up and walked down the stairs.

One day I realized Victor never left the top step the first time I went downstairs in the morning. He waited for me to remember whatever it was and walked down with me the second time.

Even the law realizes the incredible bond between people and their dogs. "Strict liability" is a lawyer's way of describing when a person is responsible for causing an injury, no matter what their excuse may be. Strict liability means you're buying the expensive lamp your kids knocked over and broke when they wouldn't stop monkeying around in the boutique shop where you probably shouldn't have brought them. In most jurisdictions, "strict liability" attaches to the owner of a dog for the actions of the dog. That dog bite case I worked on? The dog owners were unquestionably liable for the horrific injuries their dogs caused.

Victor has long since passed away, may his little

soul rest in peace. As I've raised my two kids, there have been many times, especially before they started talking, that I thought dogs and kids are not so different. Not because children are like dogs, but because dogs are so much like people. Just like Victor, my little ones go out into the world, reflecting the environment we have made for them. In the process of learning from each other and loving each other, our dogs become part of our families, and we become their pack.

    As an estate planner, I have a unique take on folks, and what is important to them. I have helped lots of people who only have animals, including dogs, to benefit from their estates after they are gone. I'd say it's not so uncommon anymore. Some folks follow the trend of leaving their legacy to kin, and forget about family pets. I always bring it up, just to make sure the bases are covered.

    At the end of our days, our greatest impact is rarely

measured in the wealth (or lack of wealth) we leave behind. Our pets are very much our legacy; a literal living on of our way of being. Don't forget your furry friends when you make your own final arrangements; you are the world to them, and they will be lost without you.

CHAPTER 6:

DIGITAL PROPERTY

How much of your life is digital? How many hours do you spend staring at your phone or computer everyday? How much email do you receive and send? Who has a password for that? Do you have social media accounts? What do you want to happen with those when you pass away? How many passwords would a person have to know to pay your bills and keep up with your business if you were incapacitated?

Funny, how the world has changed. The law is rushing to catch up, with states considering laws to allow executors and trustees to have electronic access to a decedent's information. Regardless of what happens with the law, it's an area in which you probably prefer to make your own choices for yourself.

Wills, trusts and powers of attorney can contain specific language addressing digital property. A person can be designated to manage digital property, and it would be useful to incorporate a separate document with passwords and distribution information. There are even options online for the storage and safekeeping of passwords. Companies like 1Password and PasswordSafe help people manage passwords and provide information to agents, executors or trustees. Legacy Locker, AssetLock, Cirrus Legacy and SecureSafe offer online account management and information for online accounts, as well as distribution of the information upon incapacity or death.

When I die, I'm going to have the Tetris theme played at my funeral, just as my coffin is being lowered into the ground.

WHEN IT TOUCHES THE GROUND, EVERYONE WILL HEAR THE SOUND OF "LINE COMPLETED."

CHAPTER 7:

DECLARATION OF AUTHORITY

> They say such nice things about people at their funerals that it makes me sad to realize that I'm going to miss mine by just a few days.
>
> Garrison Keillor

Nevada law allows a person to make a Declaration of Authority, to declare who should have the legal right to make decisions about your funeral arrangements. This document, even more than others, demonstrates the fact that most of your planning is not actually for your benefit; it's for those left behind.

If there's going to be a disagreement, even just a

small one, it's going to begin with the funeral director. The funeral director is the kind and sensitive person who has to get "next-of-kin" to sign a death certificate and make important decisions about preparations and funeral. When there is a disagreement among the next-of-kin, and no written direction otherwise, the funeral director can get caught in the middle of the tug-of-war. When you designate one person to make those decisions, the first and immediate concerns of burial or cremation can be allowed to happen without any drama or hold up.

> Cremation is my last hope for
> a hot, smoking body.

As for your final disposition, there are so many options and, at least in Nevada, the sky is the limit. Burial and cremation are still the most common. Liquefaction is the next wave in final disposition; there are a couple machines in the United States already. More and more people are planning "green" funerals. It may not be "fun," but it is amazing the options available, and the detail that can be covered in a meeting with a funeral director who offers pre-planning services.

The cost of funeral services, whether it's just cremation or a big show, is always cheaper "pre-need" versus "in-need." Many planning instruments will lock in the price for you. I've seen plans that even incorporate a life insurance aspect – so that if it's not paid off when you pass away, the plan pays itself off.

It's so easy to take the burden off your family and the funeral director. Appointing one person to be in charge of working with the funeral director relieves the funeral director of any potential disputes. Planning and paying ahead will result in a huge cost-saving benefit, and relieve your loved ones from the stress and emotional burden of planning your funeral on the fly.

CHAPTER 8:

FINANCIAL POWERS OF ATTORNEY

Nevada's attorneys catch a huge break when it comes to the financial and healthcare powers of attorneys; the legislature writes the form, and requires everyone to use it. Anyone can find it in Nevada statutes at NRS 162A.620. The form, like the rest of a Nevada estate plan, is completely portable to other states, and always operates under Nevada law, no matter where it goes – you can live in another state and travel among other jurisdictions without having any concern about how it impacts your documents.

The financial power of attorney allows you to name

a person, an "agent," to be in charge of your financial affairs if you ever become incapacitated. But it's no longer valid if you die. A lot of folks mistakenly believe they can rely on a power of attorney after someone passes away; that is simply not the case. The powers you grant in a power of attorney die with you.

Our Nevada form lists the specific powers so you can see how broad the power of attorney can be:

- Real Property
- Tangible Personal Property
- Stocks and Bonds
- Commodities and Options
- Banks and Other Financial Institutions
- Safe Deposit Boxes
- Operation of Entity or Business
- Insurance and Annuities
- Estates, Trusts and Other Beneficial Interests

- Legal Affairs, Claims and Litigation
- Personal Maintenance
- Benefits from Governmental Programs or Civil or Military Service
- Retirement Plans
- Taxes

Most of the time, in estate planning, a person will grant all these authorities to their agent.

You also have a choice about when the power you grant is effective. Your financial power of attorney can either be "durable" or "springing." If the power of attorney is durable, that means your agent can exercise their authority anytime after you sign it, and until you die or revoke it. For a long time, these durable powers were necessary for "non-traditional" couples; banks and other institutions will honor a marriage without any evidence that it exists, but it was not always so with unmarried couples. A durable financial power of attorney is an effective way to show third parties that you want another person to have authority to handle your personal financial matters.

A "springing" power of attorney is dormant when you sign it, but "springs to life" when you become incapacitated. With a springing power of attorney, your agent must get a written medical opinion from a licensed medical doctor saying that you are disabled or incapacitated and unable to make your own decisions with respect to financial matters. In my experience, I have noticed that a springing power of attorney is preferred by unmarried people, or people who have some uncertainty about their choice of agent.

I use a story of my own experience to illustrate the significant difference for my clients between durable and springing. Before we were married, my spouse and I had durable powers of attorney for each other. During law school, I travelled to another state one summer for an internship. One day, my spouse and agent under my financial power of attorney called to tell me we bought a car. She was able to use the power of attorney to finance a vehicle in my name, and add my name to the title. In my case, it was a relief to be able to have made the purchase without any time, effort or inconvenience to me; but it's easy to see how such power might be abused.

Nevada's statutory form also provides you with an opportunity to grant so-called "specific authorities":

- Create, amend, revoke or terminate an family, living, irrevocable or revocable trust
- Make a gift, subject to the limitations of Nevada law and any special instructions in this Power of Attorney
- Create or change rights of survivorship
- Create or change a beneficiary designation
- Waive the principal's right to be a beneficiary of a joint and survivor annuity, including a survivor benefit under a retirement plan
- Exercise fiduciary powers that the principal has authority to delegate
- Disclaim or refuse an interest in property, including a power of appointment

As you can see, these specific authorities give someone else the legal right to change significant aspects of your estate plan. Some or all of these may make sense in certain circumstances, but these authorities do not make sense in every situation. Your attorney can help you understand how they fit your circumstances.

On Nevada's form, you also have an opportunity to provide any special instructions. I've seen some really helpful information on these forms; for example, information about Aflac or another disability-type policy so your agent knows to submit a claim if you're incapacitated; information about disability-type benefits on credit cards, etc. Even information about where to find financial information or records can be helpful.

If your relationship is the kind that runs deep, but you can't or don't want to formalize that for whatever reason, a durable financial power of attorney can give each other authority to act for the other. If you are the kind of person that is not comfortable with conceding any control unless it is necessary, the springing power will give you peace of mind that you are in control, and when the time comes, someone you choose will be in control. However you use it, a financial power of attorney lets you decide how things will be addressed for you if you can't speak for yourself.

CHAPTER 9:

HEALTHCARE POWERS OF ATTORNEY

Two buddies, Bob and Earl, were two of the biggest baseball fans in America. Their entire adult lives, Bob and Earl discussed baseball history in the winter, and they poured over every box score during the season.

They went to sixty games a year. They even agreed that whoever died first would try to come back and tell the other if there was baseball in heaven.

One summer night, Bob passed away in his sleep after watching a Yankee victory earlier in the evening. He died happy. A few nights later, his buddy, Earl, awoke to the sound of Bob's voice from beyond. "Bob, is that you?" Earl asked.

"Of course it me," Bob replied.

"This is unbelievable!" Earl exclaimed. "So tell me, is there baseball in heaven?"

"Well, I have some good news and some bad news for you. Which do you want to hear first?"

> "Tell me the good news first."
>
> "Well, the good news is that, yes, there is baseball in heaven, Earl."
>
> "Oh, that is wonderful! So what could possibly be the bad news?"
>
> "You're pitching tomorrow night."

I can't tell you who to pick for your agent, but you should pick someone who cares about you, and who will be calm and serene while you face severe medical injury, illness or death.

Funny thing about health care powers of attorney – the law that allows us to identify an agent to act on our behalf is very old law. It's developed now for centuries, and its rules have not changed much to this day. One of the old rules of agency law is that if you become incapacitated, your appointment becomes invalid. Obviously, that works against the very purpose of a healthcare power of attorney, and for that reason, a healthcare power of attorney should specifically declare that it is not affected by your subsequent incapacity.

It is also very old law that invalidates your appointment of an agent upon your death. Interestingly, a well-drafted health care power of attorney will indicate it grants authority to make medical decisions for you before or after your death. Not only does emergency medicine continue to save more and more of us from the brink of death, death is manipulated in some medical procedures by freezing the body to stop the heart during surgery and subsequently reviving the patient.

In Nevada, we also use Health Care Powers of Attorney to make statements about our end of life care. Our statute provides 5 options under a section named "Statement of Desires":

1. To be kept alive at all costs, no matter what, and that your providers continually maintain your life to whatever standard possible.

2. To stop life-sustaining procedures if you are in a coma, and your doctor certifies that you have no reasonable hope of long-term recovery or survival.

3. To stop life-sustaining procedures if you have an incurable or terminal condition, and your doctor certifies that you have no reasonable hope of long-term recovery or survival. You can choose either or both of 2 and 3, but if you do, you should complete a Living Will.

If you choose not to decide, you still have made a choice: that's the option numbered "5" in Nevada's form. It's a nice statement that your agent is to run a cost-benefit analysis, and they have the authority to stop life-sustaining treatment when the burdens of treatment outweigh the benefits.

I typically advise folks that if they affirmatively choose 2 and/or 3, not to select option 5. If you know you want life sustaining treatment to stop when you have no reasonable hope of recovery or survival, then you don't have to give anyone else authority to make that decision. By making those selections, you take the burden off anyone else having to make such a choice, and you take accountability for the decision if the time comes. There is another reason I advise against granting another person the authority to make decisions regarding life-sustaining treatment.

Once upon a time (this is a true story, though facts and names are fudged to protect the innocent), a married couple were driving down a wide suburban street, having a heated argument in their car. The man driving, consumed with rage, made a hard turn and slammed the vehicle into a phone pole. Both were seriously injured, but the woman in the passenger seat was not as injured as her husband. He was in a coma; she was out of the emergency room within a matter of hours. As soon as she could, she showed their health care power of attorney to his doctors which established her authority to make decisions for him about life sustaining treatment, and she told them to pull the plug. The man's family hired a lawyer right away, and then she got a lawyer, and they were all set to go to court for a hearing within days. A few days after the accident, while the whole family was at court waiting for their hearing to start, the man woke up, all alone.

If he had made the decision for himself, and not left anyone with any authority, the man's doctors would not have to be caught in the middle of a whacko family dispute. Everyone would have had to wait an appropriate time for his recovery, and he might've woken up to his family.

The choice of agent deserves the same careful

consideration as your choice of executor.

What happened to Nevada's option 4 under "Statement of Desires"? It applies if you choose any of 2, 3 or 5, and for many people it's the toughest part of preparing an estate plan.

Nevada wants you to know: "Withholding or withdrawal of artificial nutrition and hydration may result in death by starvation or dehydration." And then you have a choice: "I want to continue receiving nutrition and hydration after all other life sustaining treatment has been withheld." I used to get thirsty just reading it.

The fact is, the time between stopping life-sustaining treatment and the end of life, is that the end of life is often hastened along with a comfortable, loving dose of morphine. Most folks pass within hours of the machines stopping. Most folks don't feel too hungry or thirsty, or anything else, I imagine.

I also know that continuing nutrition and hydration, in some circumstances, can prolong life indefinitely. Terry Schaivo was one such individual who made national headlines.

Mrs. Schaivo at 27 years old, collapsed in her home one day in 1990 in full cardiac arrest. She suffered severe brain damage due to a lack of oxygen, and after 10 weeks in a coma, was diagnosed as being in a "persistent vegetative state." After 8 years and several failed attempts to bring Mrs. Schaivo back to consciousness, Mr. Schaivo asked the county court to order that the feeding tube be removed. Mrs. Schaivo's parents, the Schindlers, opposed Mr. Schaivo in court, and the case was heard and appealed several times. At one point during the seven years of litigation, President George W. Bush returned to Washington, D.C. to sign legislation aimed at keeping Mrs. Schaivo alive.

To me, the worst part of the story is that the feeding tube stopped on March 18, 2005, and she expired March 31, 2005. That's a long time, and very likely uncomfortable and even painful. So far as I know, Oregon is the only state that recognizes a "right to die," but even Nevada allows you to ask that, when life-sustaining treatment stops, you receive medication to alleviate pain and suffering "even if it dulls my consciousness and indirectly shortens my life."

There is a section of the statutory form for a person to write in other statements or desires. People have all kinds of thoughts about their dying moments. They want to allow certain family members time to be with them before their life ends. Some people want a certain ambience. Some people have a good sense of humor:

> While incapacitated, please give me an hour in the sauna every other day, that I might be a steamed vegetable. On non-sauna days, ask me a series of difficult questions, that I might be grilled.

HIPAA is a funny law. In the scope of your estate plan, you have to give someone authority to have access to your medical information if you want them to have it, in addition to nominating your agent. Some estate planners incorporate a HIPPA release in their Healthcare power of attorney document; others prepare a separate HIPAA release. Neither is the right way; either is fine, as long as a HIPAA release is made. Without it, your health care agent would not have authority to review your medical records or discuss your medical information with your doctor. HIPAA was passed as a law to address the availability and breadth of group health plans and certain individual health insurance policies. It amended the Employee Retirement Income Security Act, the Public Health Service Act, and the Internal Revenue Code. There is a lot of commentary regarding the "unintended consequences" of medical

privacy laws. It's still affecting the way we prepare estate plans, 18 years later.

CHAPTER 10:

LIVING WILL

> Three buddies died in a car accident and went to heaven. They were asked, "When you were in your casket, and friends and family were mourning over you, what would you have liked them to say about you?"
>
> The first guy said, "I would have liked to hear them say I was a great doctor of my time, and a great family man."
>
> The second guy said, "I would have liked to hear them say I was a wonderful husband and school teacher who made a huge difference in many children's lives."
>
> The last guy said, "I would liked to hear them say, 'Look, he's moving!'"

If you make the decision to stop life sustaining treatment, or if you've granted someone else authority to make that decision for you, you ought to complete a living will. A living will provides the specific guidelines for the cessation of life-sustaining treatment. It lists a bunch of major medical interventions, and allows you to say you don't want them done for you if you have no reasonable hope for long term survival.

A living will can also have words of comfort for your family, letting them know your decision is made after careful consideration, and that your choice is based on your strong convictions and beliefs. Remember, this document will be heard in your voice at a time when no one can hear your voice. There is nothing inappropriate about expressions of love and comfort in a living will.

It should also have words of comfort for your doctor, by holding harmless the person who withholds treatment.

Nevada offers a free service through the Secretary of State called the "Living Will Lockbox." It's an electronic database accessible by medical providers; it allows your doctor to find out if you have a living will at a time when you might not be able to say. The registered document can give reference information to another person, such as your attorney, to allow a provider to track down other important documents. In the past, people would make their documents discoverable by recording them with the county public recorder. The living will lockbox is a great way to "leave breadcrumbs" without compromising the privacy of your estate plan documents.

> Last night, my kids and I were sitting in the living room and I said to them, "I never want to live in a vegetative state, dependent on some machine and fluids from a bottle. If that ever happens, pull the plug." They got up, unplugged the computer and threw out my wine.

CHAPTER 11:

SIGNED & SEALED

> On the way home from the Ash Wednesday service a young boy asked his mother, "Is it true, Mommy, that we are made of dust?"
>
> "Yes, darling."
>
> "And do we go back to dust again when we die?"
>
> "Yes, dear."
>
> "Wow!" said the boy. "When I said my prayers last night and looked under the bed, I found someone who is either coming or going!"

There are three rules I impose upon anyone who will listen. Don't sign anything, including estate plan documents, unless:

1. You've read it completely,

2. You understand it, and

3. You completely agree with it.

That's the responsibility that comes with the freedom to contract. So far, the government has not taken away your right to make decisions for yourself and appoint agents if you can't make your own choices. And so far, you still have the right to decide who, if anyone, will benefit from the physical possessions and assets you leave behind.

> The pope and a lawyer are on the elevator to heaven. When they arrive at the gates, there's a mad rush of angels, saints, and other holy people on their way to greet them.
>
> When they arrive, they pick the lawyer up on their shoulders and carry him off cheering hysterically. The pope is deeply saddened.
>
> St. Peter sees this and goes over to him and says, "Don't feel bad. We get popes in here all the time, it's not every day we get a lawyer."

Finding a lawyer to work with is your first step, and it's not always so simple. There are as many styles of legal service as there are attorneys. It's important to work with someone who you believe genuinely understands and cares about your situation.

Perhaps the greatest value in preparing your estate plan with a good attorney is the role the attorney will have with your loved ones when you pass away. Your attorney may be called on to provide documents, and if your loved ones so choose, may hire your attorney to assist with any property transfers. It's worth consulting with or interviewing multiple attorneys to find one you "click" with.

It's also important to work with an attorney who is familiar with estate planning for other folks in your situation. Mom & Pop can get the same fancy trust with all the bells and whistles that the "Rockefellers" have… but that may have expensive unintended consequences. The Rockefellers may wish to save some money on the front-end with a simple will and no tax planning, but a simple will isn't going to address all the ins and outs of a large taxable estate.

Whoever you work with, once you have everything signed and done, you will feel such a relief to have it completed. At least, that's what my clients tell me.

The Appendix has a little form to help you start

thinking about the major aspects of planning your estate, which you can use to start your discussion with your attorney. You will also find a Glossary of terms used in this book, and in estate planning literature and forms.

APPENDIX: ESTATE PLAN WORKSHEET

Circle One: Will   or   Trust

Executor / Trustee

1_____

_____ (Name)

2_____

_____ (Name)

3._____

_____ (Name)

Distribution

_____

_____

_____

_____

Declaration of Authority

Estate Plan Worksheet

1._____

_____ (Name)

2._____

_____ (Name)

3._____

_____ (Name)

Financial POA

1._____

_____ (Name)

2._____

_____ (Name)

3._____

_____ (Name)

Health Care POA

1._____

_____ (Name)

2._____

_____ (Name)

3._____

_____ (Name)

Homestead   Y   N

Real Properties

_____

_____

_____

Beneficiary Deeds

1._____

Estate Plan Worksheet
_____ (Name)

2._____

_____ (Name)

3._____

_____ (Name)

Other

_____

_____

_____

_____

_____

_____

_____

_____

_____

_____

Estate Plan Worksheet

GLOSSARY

- **Administration**

    The process of distributing the assets of an estate or trust.

- **Annuity**

    A form of insurance or investment entitled the investor to a series of annual payments.

- **Assets**

    Property owned by a person or trust, regarded as having value and available to meet debts, commitments or legacies.

- **Beneficiary**

    A person who derives advantage from something, especially a trust, will, or life insurance policy.

- **Decedent**

    A person who has died.

- **Deed**

    n. A legal document that is signed and delivered, especially one regarding the ownership of property or legal rights.

v. To convey or transfer (property or rights) by legal deed.

- **Declaration of Authority**

    Document recognized by Nevada law to appoint someone to make decisions regarding burial, cremation and funeral arrangements.

- **Estate**

    Assets belonging to an individual or trust.

- **Estate tax**

    A tax levied on the net value of the estate of a deceased person before distribution to the heirs.

- **Executor**

    A person or institution appointed by a testator to carry out the terms of their will.

- **Homestead**

    A person's or family's residence, which comprises the land, house, and outbuildings, and in most states is exempt from forced sale for collection of debt.

- **HIPPA**

HIPAA is the federal Health Insurance Portability and Accountability Act of 1996. The primary goal of the law is to make it easier for people to keep health insurance, protect the confidentiality and security of healthcare information ad help the healthcare industry control administrative costs.

- **Living will**

  A written statement detailing a person's desires regarding their medical treatment in circumstances in which they are no longer able to express informed consent, especially an advance directive.

- **Per Stirpes**

  An estate of a decedent is distributed per stirpes if each branch of the family is to receive an equal share of an estate.

- **Power of Attorney or POA**

  The authority to act for another person in specified or all legal or financial matters.

- **Probate**

  The official proving of a will.

- **Trust**

  A trust is an agreement where the trustee holds the legal possession of a fund or assets that belong to another person, the beneficiary, and it is created while the person is alive.

- **Springing trust**

    A trust that is dormant until it is needed, as defined by its own terms.

- **Irrevocable trust**

    A trust that can't be modified or terminated without the permission of the beneficiary. The grantor, having transferred assets into the trust, effectively removes all of his or her rights of ownership to the assets and the trust.

- **Trustee**

    An individual person or member of a board given control or powers of administration of property in trust with a legal obligation to administer it solely for the purposes specified.

- **Will**

    A legal document in which a person states who should receive his or her possessions after he or she dies.

www.ingramcontent.com/pod-product-compliance
Lightning Source LLC
Chambersburg PA
CBHW030910180526
45163CB00004B/1779